PRAYING EFFECTIVELY AT SOURCE

By

Gwendolyn Smith

A 7-Key Prayer Plan for Breakthrough

Praying Effectively At Source

Published by **Sheba Publications**, July 2016

Acknowledgement

I thank God for the experiences He permitted me to go through so that I can write with the conviction that He gives divine protection equal to our testing for service.

God enabled me through testing to understand the power of strategic praying. The effectiveness of this level of authority cannot be underestimated or discounted as merely tampering with the spirit realm causing a person unnecessary problems.

To whom much has been given much more is required of them. What we experience as Christians is not just for our benefit but when we can permit the pain to work for us, the experience will heal many others.

The call to destiny can drive one into the most lonely and misunderstood 'emotional' wilderness, but God's Word sustains when the climate is not conducive to fulfilling your purpose.

TABLE OF CONTENTS

PREFACE

This booklet is intended to help those who need a prayer resource to become strengthened in their spiritual walk. It is a good prayer toolkit accompanying the Word, particularly for those on the first rung of the deliverance and prayer training ministry. These same principles can develop one for an advance deliverance ministry.

The material has helped me in preparation for a strategic global reconciliation and healing ministry, and I am sure you will find its content useful to extrapolate from. It is just a model based on a personal *7-Fold Prayer Strategy.*

It highlights the key areas to consider when preparing to undertake a spiritually combative level of praying against the opponent. It is the Spirit and the Word that interfaces with the enemy and challenges the forces of evil to flee in seven different directions, affecting a process of real change.

INTRODUCTION

Do you often wonder whether God is really hearing you when you pray? When you pray there seem to be little or no progress in your efforts? There is a long wait for a response from God and you wonder - "where is God"?

Could it be that you are expecting God to answer you in a particular way? If your need is not met in that way you unconsciously overlook the response from Him.

"For Yahweh hears the needy..." (Psalms 69:33). There is no doubt that God is listening and taking note of the requests we make through prayer. When we pray, God hears us for the spirit intercedes on our behalf before the Father. If the answer seems delayed, we are instructed to wait on the Lord. As we wait, we must have a positive disposition of thankfulness and expectancy that He will come through on our behalf no matter how long it takes. It is the wait on God that is most testing of our character and attitude towards trusting our Father who loves and desires the best for

us. *"Beloved, I pray that all may go well with you and that you may be in good health, as it goes well with your soul,"(3 John 1:2).* These are God's words, and they are as credible as the day that they were ushered from the presence of God and penned by the Apostle to his beloved fellow worker Gaius.

Why will He come through for you? Because The Word is Jesus and He cannot lie. *"They that wait upon the Lord, He will renew their strength and give them their meat in due season," (Isaiah 40"31).*

CHAPTER ONE
SPIRITUAL CAPTIVITY

1.1   NATIVE SOIL OF SIN

Throughout the biblical history of man, people have faced moments of pertinent questioning as to why prevailing situations continue to plague their lives. It is no less the case today. People, families, and nations continue to experience the same generational problems. It would seem that these problems are set in motion by the sins of one generation and time-released to the next causing reoccurring problems spanning the ages.

One only has to look at the first few chapters of Genesis to see how the social anthropology of man reveals the same patterns of sinful behavioural traits across ensuing generations. These endemic offenses are spiritually rooted in the fall of Adam, our forefather. They are lawful curses spiritually derived from the human lineage through disobedience.

Therefore, it requires strategic spiritual keys to unlock and eradicate the problems from our lives.

Why are these curses lawful? It is because sins have been committed. These entrance points of sin remain open from one generation to another. Cultural norms have bound many into acceptable traits and behaviours that are against the laws of God. Even when the Spirit convicts people of their sins, they remain in rebellion. Their actions and ways become sins of iniquity passed down through the familial and cultural lineage. The spiritual door remains open, because they have not confessed and repented to God.

Sin is a strong innate impulse in man. We can sin without effort. It is a spiritual drive in the makeup of man to sin. Biologically, a "drive" is a physiological urge to bring satisfaction to the body's need. If someone is thirsty, the body is designed to signal that desire for water. The symptoms of thirst are abated when the need is met. Physiological drives are strong urges, and they elicit a response to be satisfied. The compelling impulse in us to disobey God is driven by Satan's intent to deceive us. It is a very strong urge. Without divine grace, we will sin without compunction. Our relationship with God was compromised in Adam's fall from grace. In essence, we are carriers of the spiritual defect in the eternal gene pool of mankind.

The end portion of Psalms 69:33 "*...and does not despise his captive people,*" gives a scriptural clue as to why we experience so much difficulty. The word "captive" is the active word. The human race is fundamentally defected by sin. So is the foundational order of human living as set by God. People are spiritually tied and held in bondage even when they desire spiritual liberty. Spiritual captivity holds people, families, communities, and nations against their will, to prevent them from finding restoration and healing in Jesus. National customs, ancestry and religions can predispose people to a cultural norm of thinking, understanding, and believing.

These embedded features of ethnic traits have an impact on our cognition and can be a determining factor to how receptive we are to God's Word. When social norms conflict with the Word, it can hinder spiritual understanding of God and how He works with humankind. It is the role of the Holy Spirit to bring spiritual enlightenment and release men from these collective bondages.

1.2   THE TEMPTER

After Jesus had fasted 40 days and night, His body was physically weak and His mental and emotional states would have been vulnerable. As part of Jesus' preparation for his Messianic ministry, He would face His hour of severe temptation in the desert. Satan approaches the Son of God, firstly, to tempt Him to turn stones into bread and to eat knowing that He was naturally hungry.

Secondly, he coaxes Jesus into jumping from the pinnacle of the temple into the bustling courtyard below and thirdly, Satan takes Jesus to a high mountain position to show Him all the kingdoms of the world. He blatantly offers them to Jesus knowing the Word that they belong to the Son of God. Now, why would he be so bold and audaciously conniving? Because this is the same spirit that challenged God and took a third of the angelic host of heaven into the spiritual abyss with him. The word "if" is a conjunction forming two statements. Clearly his statements are loaded and in essence, this is what Satan is proposing to Jesus. "If you are who you say you are then demonstrate your power before the people and worship me." Jesus rebuked Satan by quoting the Word *"...Get thee hence, Satan: for it is written, thou shalt worship the Lord thy God, and him only shalt thou serve,"* *(Matthew 4:10 KJV).* Now let us look further at the spirit behind that statement.

Satan is the tormentor of human situations. He uses the force of the spiritual law to entrap the people in bondage. Satan is the accuser of the people, and as a skilled arbitrator, he will use the breadth of his legal powers to implicate God's people. Remember the episode in Exodus, the standoff as he argued his case for Moses' body. The temerity of this spirit that knows no bounds to ingeniously argue the legality of our actions in light of God's Word. The adversary will form a judgement against God's people based on pure conjecture, but he uses the Word deceitfully as the basis of his summation.

Satan uses his legal knowledge of the Word to keep one entrenched in fear and ignorance concerning the power of the same Word to deliver. When you come to the full knowledge of the truth concerning the potency of the Word, the strength of Satan's power is obliterated. He has no power unless given by God. The awesome power of love breaks the proverbial "chains" around the hearts and minds and renders them powerless in the glorious face of our Lord. We become liberated from the bondage of collective captivity, cultural ties, hereditary predispositions, religious fallacy, familial limitations, and generational strongholds.

The Adversary is against God's people. He does not want people to come to the knowledge of God's truth. In your struggles of life, there is an advocate in the person Jesus Christ who lovingly and compassionately restores and rebuilds the lives of those who have crashed into the buffers of life. There are many, like myself who are witnesses of Jesus' power to heal and recover all from life's pitfalls. *"He sent His word and healed them; He rescued them from the pit,"* (Psalms 107:20 *(Holman's Christian Standard Bible)*. We advocate His Lordship in our lives to rescue us from problems and His ability to deliver us from all evil strongholds. There are expressions of inner joy to celebrate our new perspective on life through the transformational love of Jesus.

1.3 FAMILIAL STRONGHOLDS

We will now discuss some problematic situations that are potentially deep rooted. A deeply embedded habitual problem is an indication that there is an area of your life that has become a stronghold of the enemy. There are many ways in which one can become vulnerable, weak or even predisposed to a particular problem or situation. Let us look at two types of generational factors and predispositions. When we are born, we do not come into life as a clean sheet as many would hope. Parental lifestyles, gene pools and cultures can all play a role in your pre-natal and post-natal life. Let us put together two hypothetical case studies for thought.

Case Study 1:

"He heals the brokenhearted and binds up their wounds" (Psalms 147:3 ESV).

This case highlights what I believe could constitute a generational predisposition.

Olivier is two years old. He was born affected by a number of recurring setbacks to his health. Olivier's mother, Debra was a chronic drug user and from the age of 14 years, she has tried to give up the habit unsuccessfully.

Pathological results showed that Debra's immune system is severely weak resulting from a number of medical issues. She is now on medication to sustain her long-term recovery from the effects of her earlier life choices. Debra's own health challenges have severely affected Olivier's immune system. His health has been severely impaired, affecting his life chances. Now 34 years old, Debra is mindful of the inherent problems Olivier is facing.

Debra has now matured as a person and is committed to the wellbeing of her young child. However, the effects of years of chronic drug abuse have taken their toll on her body and state of mind. During the pregnancy, she underwent therapy and treatment to prepare her for her new role as a mother. Debra hoped then that the interventions would somehow lessen the problems Olivier would inherit. Sadly, that was not the case.

It is clear in the overview of Case Study 1 that Debra's early lifestyle of drug abuse had an impact on her health thereby predisposing Olivier to a weakened immune system and other medical challenges. She unwittingly gave an entrance to drug abuse. Unless the door is closed through the deliverance prayer ministry, which goes to the root of the problem, it is likely that the next generation will easily succumb to taking drugs.

Sadly, Debra is now faced with raising a child whose health needs will place great demands on her to give the best quality of life to her son. No one accounts for life's setbacks when they are young and have many choices to be made. The reality, however, sets in motion a cycle of time-transferring generational penalties. Sadly, sometimes there is a price to pay for the mistakes that we make in life even when we have come to know the Lord. Facing the consequences of the choices we make in life is a burden that we must bear. God gives us the grace to learn from life's experiences that will benefit those who cross our path in life.

The cause and effect of why Debra pursued an excessively indulgent lifestyle is yet another chapter to her case study. However, it is not unusual for young people to over-identify with experimentation within their peer groups. But, it is clear that she pushed the boundaries of what appeared to be a normal conservative upbringing. Herein lies the clue to the root of her self-destructive behaviour. She revealed her need to rebel against conservatism and parental expectations for her life.

Her choices may be as a result of her inability to project her unique self and therefore, her self-inadequacies plagued her fragile self-esteem. During her final years in school, Debra's bright, promising, educational future was threatened by her drug use. She carried the burden of letting down her parents and her guilt was overwhelming. She said, "I had to break away from family expectations and think about me. At that time in my life, it is what I wanted to do." Clearly, there was nothing wrong with her upbringing, but she was rebelling against it. In order to understand her frustrations one would need to probe more. The mother-child tie that can be stifling needs to be broken.

Case Study 2:

"You, LORD, brought me up from the realm of the dead; you spared me from going down to the pit," (Psalms 30:3, NIV).

Here is a theoretical case of what could constitute a family curse indicating a generational stronghold.

Charles and Nigel are brothers who grew up in a relatively happy home environment. They were educated at private prep schools and went on to the local village high school. They both achieved good school and college grades and went on to university where they both excelled in their chosen educational paths.

With excellent passes, Charles went on to study law ending up in a prestigious barristers' chamber. Nigel, on the other hand, studied pharmacy and went to America to finish a Ph.D. before landing himself a job in a reputable research laboratory.

Ten years later, Charles and Nigel meet up once again, this time at their father's funeral. Their father committed suicide. The family is devastated but the sombre atmosphere is eerily reminiscent of a previous family gathering a few years earlier when their uncle, John also committed suicide. In fact, the family history on their father's side is a catalogue of suicides and unexplained sudden or tragic deaths. For Charles and Nigel, this is not comforting. With reassuring hugs from their inconsolable mother, they put on a brave face.

Many years later, the fate of Charles is poignantly sealed when after a bitter divorce and losing custody of his children, he contemplated the unthinkable and walked away from life. One evening, the call came through to Nigel that Charles' body was found under a bridge at low tide. The generational curse had struck the family yet again.

Family life is tested by the "peaks and troughs" of experiences encountered. We learn to weather the storms and carry on regardless of prevailing circumstances. Many people accept recurring unexplained incidences as normal. The experiences of the family in hypothetical case study two may therefore seem to be a natural course of life events albeit tragic episodes for the family. For those who understand the strategic spiritual influences over nations, communities, ministries, families and marriages, it is clear that there is an evil spiritual activity at work in the life of this family.

A generational iron grip of evil has strengthened through the years. You will know it is a curse because it is reoccurring problem. This invasive occupation is actively at work aborting lives. In this case, it is manifested through suicides, and the sudden unexplained demise of family members across the generations. It is undoubtedly an inherited curse, spiritually bequeathed, it appears to work through the male lineage. It is a legacy of premature or untimely deaths, and the spiritually enforcing powers must be broken at source in order to see a change of outcome in the ensuing generations.

Whatever iniquities or covenants with death that the ancestors have entered into must be destroyed through the Potentate of our faith the Lord Jesus Christ. Our Lord has the authority over all realms of evil to heal our families and restore life.

1.4   A NATURE TO SIN

Since we are of the gene pool of Adam and Eve we are fundamentally flawed. The spiritual structure of our being has been morally corrupted by their sin. Inherent sins through disobedience have led us away from the protective presence of God where we are empowered by the Spirit to overcome the challenges we face. It is the strategy of the enemy to use the mind to bring about his desired intent to destroy people.

As human beings, we are weak against spiritual attacks without the divine assistance of our Lord. The areas of life where individuals or families are prone to experience failures are known to the enemy. Armed with that information, Satan will launch an attack against the mind by implanting a lie or a deeply embedded destructive behaviour pattern. So strong are these attacks that many people find themselves bound by a hopeless and lamentable cycle of helplessness. It is a pitiable state to be in, unable to break free from the clutches of evil. The person knows that their lifestyle or thinking is destructive, yet, they are unable to change their behaviour. They are drawn into a downward spiral of self-destruction.

1.5   HELP IN THE WORD

Be assured, you are not a hopeless case. There is no benefit in self-berating or condemnation by others.   Life is for learning, and you can pick up the pieces in a positive way that will benefit others. There is help from the Word of God.   One does not become bound simply because it just happens. No! It is because there has been a failure on our part to address areas of our lives where we continually fall short. Over time, the spirits that control those areas of our lives strengthen their grip, and we become powerless to resist them. Just as Jesus used the Word to overcome the enemy, so you will have to be disciplined in using the Word to begin to take back your spiritual territories. There is no victory without a fight! It will be a spiritual battle using the Word to pray in order to change your situation.

Use these *seven simple steps* to begin to change your life:-

> *1.*   Firstly, admit your problem openly. The enemy has no control over you when you choose not to be silent about your problem.   Give it to Jesus and disown it at the cross. *"Therefore, confess your sins one to another and pray one for one*

another, that you may be healed. The prayer of a righteous person has great power as it is working," (James 5:16, ESV).

2.   Secondly, pray and ask God to forgive you of your sins. Ask Jesus to reveal to you how the doors to the habitual sins were open, ie, lifestyle, generational sins, disobedience etc. *"If we confess our sins, he is faithful and just to forgive us of our sins and to cleanse us from all unrighteousness,"* (1 John 1:9, ESV)

3.   Thirdly, forgive those you may be holding responsible for the failure of your life. It is said that the *bravest* person is the first to offer an apology to another. The first to forgive is the *stronger* one and the person who forgets is the *happiest*. *"For if you forgive men when they sin against you, your heavenly Father will also forgive you. But if you do not forgive men their sins, your Father will not forgive your sins,"* (Matthew 6:14-15, NIV)

4.	Find the scriptural verses for your situation. Allow the Spirit to direct you into the Word. You may need to get help from someone who is familiar with the scriptures if you are not.

5.	Pray the scriptural verses three times a day personalising the Word to your needs. You will know when you have the victory over the problem and no further prayer is required in that area.

6.	Believe and thank God that His Word is working for you as you walk by faith turning away from doing the things you do habitually.

7.	Continue to thank God even for incremental steps towards recovery. Ask His forgiveness when you slip up as you take each daily step of faith.

Being persistent and disciplined in your prayer life will help you to gain the spiritual strength to win the turf war.

1.6   TURF WAR

Your life can be likened to a parcel of ground. If you do not have a personal relationship with Jesus or as a Christian you are careless in tending your ground, it will be overgrown with weeds. In this case, the weeds are synonymous with the sins present in our lives. When the ground is overgrown, the hardy spiritual weeds will proliferate across your land choking the healthy aspects of your life.

When we begin to pray and actively pursue the things of God pertaining to recovery and restoration of our lives, the turf war begins. Satan does not want you to clear your land from tenaciously destructive sinful roots. He is content when your hedges are broken down and the ground overgrown and untended. If you are spiritually bound, the spirit will immobilise you with fear so that you become inactive to take back your ground. You have no inclination towards cleaning up your life. You are in a spiritual state of stupor as you become sluggish in praying and being indisciplined in the Word. Satan ensures that you remain impotent and spiritually incapacitated while your life continues to spiral out of control.

It is time to get busy about your deliverance and healing. Put on the whole armour of God according to Ephesians 6:12 so that you will be spiritually equipped to fight and stand against every assault perpetrated by the enemy.

If you fall on the battlefield just get up again and keep working through the problems. During the time of engaging in your recovery, you may need to have someone in the ministry of deliverance and intercession to help you. This is important to avoid further entrapment by the enemy. However, the Spirit of God is with you from the moment you make up your mind to beseech the Lord in penitent praying. God wants to see that you are serious about recovering your spiritual grounds. His grace is sufficiently more than enough to bring you back from the brink of your despair.

1.7   A COMPASSIONATE SAVIOUR

It was for the spiritual captivity of mankind that Jesus came into this life to release into us new life. Throughout His earthly ministry, we see the dire conditions of the people and what He had to face. *"But when he saw the multitudes, he was moved with compassion for them, because they were distressed and scattered, as sheep not having a shepherd," (Matthew 9:36, ASV).* The people were bound in spiritual chains too heavy to bear and the religious leaders were uncaring. Their desperate plight moved our

Lord with divine compassion. He cared that men were suffering in the pits of despair and destruction as depicted in Psalms 107:20. It was a spiritual problem that warranted a spiritually robust response. There could be no compromise with the spirits holding the people in captivity. In His authority as Lord over evil, He gave that power to us to command that these unclean spirits come out of the people. *"And he called unto him his twelve disciples, and gave the authority over unclean spirits, to cast them out and to heal all manner of disease and all manner of sickness."* *(Matthew 10:1, ASV).*

When Jesus cast out the demon from the disturbed young man His disciples enquired as to why they were unable to cast the demon out. Jesus' response was, *"This kind can come out by nothing, save by prayer,"* *(Mark 9:29, ASV).* Now here was a case of a serious demonic stronghold over the life of this young man. There is no release from such depth of destruction except by the power of the Anointed One. It is this authority of power that has been imparted to us in the name of Jesus Christ. It requires the humbling of oneself in petition to God to help such an individual. The ordinary just will not do to release the people from the spiritual pits they have fallen into.

1.8   BREAKING CYCLES OF DEFEAT

Keeping with the above case of the disturbed young man, we can see from the scripture that it was an extremely distressing example of demonic bondage. The power of the Word is potent to destroy every negative aspect of your life. The legal arguments devised by the enemy to cause failure and disruption in your life can be countered and demolished by the Word when we pray.

"For you will break the yoke of their slavery and lift the heavy burden from their shoulders. You will break the oppressor's rod, just as you did when you destroyed the army of Midian," (Isaiah 9:4, NLT). It was Gideon who broke the cycle of defeat the Israelites were experiencing under the oppression of the Midianites. It was seven years under complete provocation that caused Gideon to rise up in the anointing to break the national bondage over the people. Satan is the oppressor, and the ultimate yoke to be broken is sin.

Jesus is the Saviour of the people chosen as the Anointed One to break every chain of demonic systems against the people. The power of our Lord is not bound nor can it be restrained in destroying every spiritual cycle of defeat one can encounter.

In order to experience freedom from collective or personal captivity, one has to exercise faith in the Word that sets men free from the bondage of sin. A spiritual bondage can be explained as every challenge we face that becomes habitual or hard to break. The individual is unable to take control of that area of their lives. However, that being said, without any deliberation, the approach to God requires a robust strategic prayer strategy.

CHAPTER TWO: STRATEGIC INTELLIGENCE

2.1 KNOWING YOUR OPPONENT

One of the most effective ways to fight in any war is to spend time gaining intelligence about your enemy. In Deuteronomy, Israel chose twelve spies to enter the land that God had promised them and to spy it out. The purpose of spying out the enemy invaded territory was to acquire gainful insight into their operations and how they are strategically organised.

This level of strategic intelligence gives the advantage to determine what is their military strength and capabilities. In a spiritual war, the operation is no less skillfully approached. Ignorance in stealth operation is not bliss, it is a deadly error. Hosea 4:6 records that because of the lack of knowledge the people perish. The verse further states that they have rejected knowledge. God gives liberally, but we must receive His knowledge from His Word and act upon it accordingly.

The Holy Spirit is the agent who empowers God's people with spiritual intelligence on the enemy's plans and covert operations against God's people. When we are sensitive to the Spirit of God, we can avoid the collateral damage intended by the enemy when he strikes.

The Holy Spirit has the perfect attributes of the seven eyes before the throne of God, *"John to the seven churches that are in Asia: Grace to you and peace from him who is and who was and who is to come, and from the seven spirits who are before his throne,"* *(Revelation 1:4, ESV).* Even Jesus needed spiritual help in His time here on earth. These seven spirits accompanied Him to accomplish the things of God according to Isaiah 9: 25. It is the role of the Spirit to forearm and forewarn God's people when they are encountering spiritual conflicts. God gives His people a word of knowledge that is information that would otherwise not have been known. The Spirit speaks what is known and is the revealer of all things.

2.2   A PROPHETIC WORD

There are a number of ways the Spirit can engage one by providing revelation and insight into how to fight a particular battle. God speaks to us through His Word. He may also reveal intelligence through dreams and visions and usually, He will confirm through others as a witness. It is in the mind of God for us to be victorious in all our battles so the Spirit will provide the spiritual intelligence needed to be successful.

The Word enables you to fight in a strategically effective manner. Jesus provides the strength to put up a resistance to the tactics employed by the enemy and his interplay to frustrate our efforts. The enemy's line of attack is to wear down God's people, relentlessly bombarding them with problems. It is the Word that renews and strengthens you to recover from every assault. You are endowed with grace with the ability to persistently and tenaciously fight the good fight of faith. We are reminded that the fight is not our fight.

King Jehoshaphat when faced with the worrying news that the three armies of Ammon, Moab and Mount Seir had encamped against his nation in the Accent of Ziz, was encouraged with these prophetic words from Jahaziel. (14) *"Listen... this is what the LORD says to you: 'do not be afraid or discouraged because of this vast army. For the battle is not yours, but God's.'"* (17) *"You will not need to fight in this battle. Stand firm, hold your position, and see the salvation of the LORD on your behalf,"* (2 Chronicles 20:17 ESV). The spiritual fight is undoubtedly the Lord's fight. It is a battle fought by our Lord and won triumphantly at the cross. God will not leave His people comfortless. When situations are overwhelming and there seems no way out of the problem, God shows up mightily on behalf of those who will seek Him. A word from God was what King Jehoshaphat needed to face his enemies.

It is a ferocious encounter between good and evil for the territory of our souls. The spiritual war will continue to rage long after our term of service has ceased on earth. We are challenged to contend for the faith that was once delivered to the saints (Jude 1:3). Such contending may cause much suffering and rejection by men who are against the work of grace. We are called to resist the works of evil for the spiritual freedom we can experience through our salvation. It requires that we remain steadfast and true to the principles of the faith as we engage in the eternal fight.

CHAPTER THREE: GENERATIONAL SINS

3.1 COVENANTS

The high and eternal priesthood of Jesus is the ministry of reconciliation. His eternal role and position are superiorly far greater than that which was under the earthly high priesthood. The Levitical order was not made obsolete but out-shadowed by the surpassing glory of the new order that came through Jesus. His law is now in the hearts of men. No longer is the law written on tablet of stones. The law, now embedded in our hearts has removed any legal intent by man to spiritually abscond from the weight of personal responsibility.

A covenant is a legally binding agreement between two or more parties stipulating the legal boundaries of the agreement. Therefore, it clearly advocates what is expected of the parties in terms of the ongoing relationship. God made a covenant with His people making it clear on tablets of stone the legal boundaries of His law to man.

In land law, there are restrictive covenants on some lands that require the owner or leaseholder to abide by the legal impositions that are stipulated. Restrictive covenants usually curtail the land usage and entitlement for the benefit of others. Our faith is not restrictive but rather, its graces are profusely overflowing to benefit others who will come to salvation. We are blessed with the promises of God when we adhere to the eternal boundaries of our faith. Everything within our entire being gives adulation and praise for the freedom we have in Christ Jesus.

It is God, the Ancient of Days who has set the spiritual boundaries for mankind. They were given to us through the Jewish teachings on matters of life, family and civil law. They have their foundations in the Ten Commandments tableau, given to Moses on Mount Sinai by God. Hence, many nations' constitutions and governance in civil laws are based on the Torah's "Written Law", particularly those of Christian foundations. In Exodus, we are warned not to remove the old landmarks. It is a legal infringement to shift the landmarks.

3.2   REMOVING OLD LANDMARKS

What do we mean by removing the old landmarks? One can draw parallels with legal land matters whereby the judiciary intervenes in land disputes. It is an infringement to violate another man's territory by moving the marked out borders. A cornerstone is erected as a legal boundary to deter stealth. Where there are disputes, the original title deed for the land settles the matter in a court of law.

Jesus is the cornerstone of our faith. What God has decreed through His Word is eternal and cannot be changed. When we meddle with His truth, we are shifting the boundary lines. We are the property of God likened to a parcel of ground. *"Or do you not know that your body is a temple of the Holy Spirit within you, whom you have from God? You are not our own,"* (1 Corinthians 6:19, ESV). It is the enemy of our faith who entices us to remove the old landmarks. Shifting the spiritual boundaries of our faith is transgressing the law of God. *"Remove not the old landmark; and enter not into the fields of the fatherless: For their Redeemer is mighty; he shall plead their cause with thee,"* (Proverbs 23:10-11, KJV).

The covenant God made with Abraham was a blessing that would pass onto all who would be born into the nation of Israel. It was for all those who would be spiritually birthed to become inheritors of the promise through Jesus. It was prophesied that Israel would become a great nation scattered on the face of the earth. It was God's intention that His people would be covenant keepers and worship His holy name before the other nations. *"You shall not worship them or serve them; for I, the Lord, your God, am a jealous God, visiting the iniquity of the fathers on the children, on the third and fourth generations of those who hate Me, but showing lovingkindness to thousands, to those who love Me and keep My commandments,"(Exodus 20:5-6, NASB)*

There were many times, however, when Israel failed miserably to do the will of God. God punished His people but continued to show His love and kindness when they repented of their sins. As a nation, Israel continued to push the boundaries of the law given to them by Moses. They were, in essence, perpetual lawbreakers and often times the landmarks of God's commandments were moved to worship other gods, inciting the wrath of God.

3.3   LEGAL IMPOSITIONS

Our relationship with God is legally binding and carries with it spiritual obligations.   For our lawful access to God and for the benefit of those who will come to Jesus, we are instructed to keep the commandments of God. The ancient covenants imposed by God for mankind are irrevocably binding because they are eternal covenants.   Covenant-breaking sets in motion a spiritually legal process with penalties if the offender does not repent. Satan comes into his own when we sin because he has the right to execute his version of punishment. *"Thou shalt not bow down thyself unto them, nor serve them: for I the LORD thy God [am] a jealous God, visiting the iniquity of the fathers upon the children unto the third and fourth [generation] of them that hate me,"(Deuteronomy 5:9, KJV).* Be assured Satan will not excuse our sins before God.   He will ensure punishment is executed.

The passage above indicates that God would inflict vengeance upon the nation when the fathers or forefathers sinned. Their failure to repent of abominable acts such as worship to other deities would invoke God's displeasure. It is a sin that God found detestable and one that caused Him to repudiate their sacrifices and offerings unless there was true forgiveness.

He would disown the children and the lineage to come because it was deemed a national failure not to pass on the covenant teachings to ensuing generations. When fathers passed on the teachings of what is morally right, the generations are blessed. Equally, when what is morally wrong is adhered to it brings a generational curse.

Clearly, we have to choose which path to follow. Our decisions in life have a profound effect on ensuing generations. Equally, we can choose to make a difference and stave the evil by resisting the sins of previous generations. Josiah was eight years old when he succeeded his father King Amon to the throne. King Amon was assassinated and during his reign, he did evil in the eyes of God.

Josiah chose to follow his forefather King David and set about destroying the high places of idol worship. *"And these words which I command you today shall be in your heart. You shall teach them diligently to your children,"* *(Deuteronomy 6:6-7)*. The righteous acts of obedience by this young boy-King would cause a national shift in a positive attitude towards worship unto God.

3.4 GENERATIONAL CONFLICT

The Israelites did evil in the eyes of the LORD, and for seven years he gave them into the hands of the Midianites. "When the Israelites saw that their situation was critical and that their army was hard pressed, they hid in caves and thickets, among the rocks, and in pits and cisterns," (1 Samuel 13:6).

In the earlier chapter of 1.8, reference was drawn to Gideon bringing deliverance to Israel from the Midianites. Now let us look at it in more depth. In Hebrew the name "Midian" means strife. God told his people not to marry or intermingle with the hostile nations around them. The relationship between Israel and the Midian nation had long been a difficult one. The story of Moses meeting and marrying Zipporah, the daughter of Jethro, a Midianite priest, is found in Exodus 2:16-22. The marriage did not placate the uneasy relationship with his wife's people and the discord at times was intensely provocative.

It was Balak, the King of Midian who objected to the Israelites passing through his land. Perturbed by this mass of people encamped on his borders he summoned the prophet Balaam to curse God's people. Balaam was forbidden by God to curse His people. God gave Balaam oracles of blessings to pronounce upon Israel. Still tempted to find a way to rid his borders of the nomadic horde, Balak and Balaam deceitfully contrived to entice Israel to eat food sacrificed to idols. Israel may have been lured into sin deceitfully but their hearts were already open to disobedience and folly as they pushed the boundaries to test the patience of God. The doorway to sin was opened through disobedience. To eat food offered to idols was abominable and it was spiritually shifting an old landmark. This act of unfaithfulness incurred the wrath of God.

If the Midianites were a people of strife then Israel was a stubborn and disobedient people. God brought judgement against His people by putting it into the heart of the Midianites to torment them. For seven years, the Midianites, Amalekites and other nomadic tribes plundered and pillaged their land. The strife with Israel would not abate as crops were taken, livestock stolen, and the land stripped bare. Seven years of provocation was a perfect state of aggravation against Israel.

This was God's judgement against His people. Transgressing the laws of God warranted His prompting to bring about the desired oppression.

CHAPTER FOUR: CHOSEN TO FIGHT

4.1   UNDER ATTACK

Those in the intercessory and deliverance ministries are called to the service of God to make a difference. They are chosen to fight for spiritually assigned territories. It is, therefore, no wonder many intercessors are under attack as the opposition seeks to frustrate and disable the ministries that bring healing to the people who are bound.

God has placed within families, churches, communities, and nations, people He has chosen to be frontline prayer intercessors. They are called to watch and pray. The gates of these entities must be manned day and night with intercessory praying. These entities must be fortified and robustly guarded. The people who God has placed in the watchtowers will experience vicious attacks from the very people they love and are commissioned to pray for.

It is an unthankful task to be called to be a restorer of the breach. However, spiritually, it is an honour to be called by God to this position of standing in the gap for those who cannot help themselves. *"Those from among you will rebuild the ancient ruins; you will raise up the age-old foundations; and you will be called the repairer of the breach. The restorer of the streets in which to dwell,"* *(Isaiah 58:12).* This verse alludes to the restoration of Jerusalem after Israel came out of captivity. The city was ruined and destroyed to its very foundations. Able men were called upon to repair the damage done by the enemies who had long gone.

Jesus was the repairer of the breach. Under His ministry of reconciliation, He restored the human race back to the Father conquering over the powers militating against the healing of the people. This great victory for mankind was secured at the cross. Jesus suffered that we might be delivered from spiritual bondage and oppression.

Today, God is raising up men and women called out to restore all entities of life back to God. Peace, joy and godly living will be the order of the day as families, ministries, communities and nations thrive under the banner of God's love. The healing waters will pour from the fountain of life springing up in the hearts of men.

The spirit of denominationalism will be broken as the Spirit brings about a true oneness in Christ Jesus. The waste and uninhabitable regions will be restored to the communities as suitable for living. Fear and the terror of evil will be abolished as this new season of reparation, social justice, reconciliation, forgiveness, and healing is ushered in.

4.2   STANDING IN THE GAP

We now understand that Gideon was the one chosen by God to stand in the gap. His assignment was to bring deliverance to his people from their relentless enemies.

In Judges 6, Gideon, busy threshing wheat in his father's winepress encountered an angel sitting under an oak tree. The angel approached him saying, "The Lord is with you, mighty warrior." The call of God usually disrupts one's life and calls you away from your old life to a new life. You are called out of your daily routines into service. Gideon, like many other biblical leaders chosen by God, questioned why they should be singled out for such an honour. They are the most unlikely people in the eyes of men. They are more than likely self-abasing individuals who feel deeply inadequate or unworthy of the assignment. This constant self-berating tendency usually serves to keep them at the feet of Jesus.

Gideon's insecurities were manifested in the need for direction and affirmation from God. In those times of uncertainty, it is paramount that divine guidance is sought particularly on those extraordinary faith journeys mapped out for those called to prophetic and apostolic assignments. Gideon, feeling inadequate for the call sought a sign that God was with him.

When God calls you, He changes your outlook on life and destiny. This juncture of lonely contemplation and surrender brings with it the reproach of men who are not privy to what God is doing. We must trust God that He is perfect in all His decisions in selecting those He will use for His service.

During a conversation with the angel, Gideon reveals his frustrations with the problem Israel was encountering as a people. The nations and tribes from the surrounding territories were pillaging the livestock and goods from God's people. Gideon was concerned that they were not seeing the intervention of God and His deliverance as their forefathers did in the wilderness.

4.3   LABOURING IN THE WINEPRESS

Winepress in scripture signifies divine judgement. The children of Israel were under God's judgement because of their sins. They were hiding in caves and under rocks. Their way of life was being affected because they were running scared from the hostile nations and nomadic tribes.

When the angel approached Gideon, it was an indication that the time to come out of the place of judgement was upon Israel. A momentously divine intervention is required when the Word is released to come forth for the one whom God chooses to stand in the gap. All of hell's power would be belched out forcibly against the people's deliverance.

The moment for Gideon to come out of a small place had come but not before the season of preparation in his family's business had come to maturity.   He had spent much time symbolically "treading the grapes" in order to release the juice that the people needed to refresh them. Now destiny and purpose were upon him to tread the battlefields to cut down the enemies of God's people. All of his fears, pains, frustrations, and discouragements experienced in that place of testing would soon be released as power. The anointing needed to destroy the enemies of God would come upon him on the battlefield. Chosen for the call, he would do exploits for God.

There are times when the circumstances of life drive us to take drastic measures to counter the effects of our enemies. Gideon and his kinfolks took action to secure their crops. Contrary to customary practices, he took to threshing wheat in a winepress.

The winepress structure is basically a fairly deep narrow pit cut out of a rock surface. It is where one would tread grapes. It would have been a confined space for threshing the stalks of wheat. The task was made harder for Gideon as the environment would have been restrictive. The feet that would tread the battlefield in an open arena are now standing in a place of confinement, a restricted winepress cut out from a rock surface. It was laboriously challenging for Gideon. No doubt, he would have stood in the same position for long hours trying to get the desired results as he would on the threshing floor. It was extremely gruelling work in the heat of the day requiring extraordinary physical strength and stamina.

4.4　THE THRESHING FLOOR EXPERIENCE

The threshing floor signifies repentance and healing. In contrast to the winepress, the threshing floor is constructed in a spacious unrestrictive area. The work of threshing wheat is done in a wide open space allowing room for the processing of the crops. It is usually an expanse of flat land, an uphill plateau so that any wind can help in the winnowing process.

Symbolically, the wind of the Spirit blows away the chaff and trash in our lives. The Word of God refines us so that we are versatile and pliable in God's hand. The stubble that falls away from us is swept away and placed on the dung heap for burning. Dung heaps are spiritually symbolic of the place of deliverance. The waste and refuse of sin are only fit to be burnt. All our ungodly and unfruitful works go through the process of being burnt by the fire of the Word for us to be purified.

The challenges that Gideon faced were in preparation for his call to fight on the behalf of his people. God loved the character of the man as he worked faithfully in his father's business. I am sure there were times he felt disillusioned and fed-up with his life's chores. However, a sense of duty kept him serving compliantly. It was a test of his attitude for service. When God chooses his servant He foreknows the heart. He would have seen from eternity the spirit of Gideon and his integrity for service. God judged Gideon to be worthy for His service long before his call came.

4.5   A STEEP LEARNING ARC

It does not matter how you have been trained in basic deliverance, ultimately it is the Spirit who educates you. Like Gideon, your personal life experiences will be the training assault course that equips you. I knew that God was calling me to a strategic dimension of spiritual warfare not encountered by many. Sure enough, the Spirit taught me how to fight, giving me the impetus to recover all entities of my life from the abyss of destruction. It was a steep curve of learning to grapple with.   However, it was indeed important for me because I had to pass the obstacle tests, otherwise, I could not go into the assignment I was called to. It is too spiritually challenging and mistakes would be too costly.

I learnt from those early spiritual encounters in the battle that the Devil's aim is to destroy me. I totally depend on the Spirit to instruct me and order my steps in the Word. After learning the basics in the deliverance ministry through a pastor in this area of ministry, I learnt to fight and develop my spiritual muscle through the wilderness experience. It was a lonely place without the help of others to bolster me up.

God, in his wisdom, set me apart on a steep learning curve in preparation for the work He has called me to. He removed everyone from me and had me all to Himself for training. It is without doubt that it is the Spirit of God who equips, trains and empowers one for the prophetic call.

4.6   TAKING CONTROL

Now that we understand how our lives can be complicated by the actions or words of previous generations, it is time to take the fight to the enemy. It is imperative for the people of God to actively engage in the good fight of faith in order to take control of our heritage. God gave his people the promise land but they had to fight in order to be inheritors with full legal right. We must occupy the length and breadth of our land until Christ comes. We must be diligent in our approach to guard and protect what has been given unto us spiritually. Our salvation was secured by the shedding of the blood of our Lord Jesus, symbolic of the sacrificial lamb.

When we come into a relationship with our Lord Jesus, we become inheritors of the promise of God. The fight has only commenced at the point of salvation but the hard work is to clean up the land or territory and make it a peaceably habitable jurisdiction where the presence of the Lord dwells. It is the Word that enables us to be bold and combative to resist against evil occupation. The Word is the legally spiritual authority that we can employ to take down all forces of evil militating against us. Our heritage in God is our rightful territory.

4.7   AN OPEN DOOR

When we sin we allow access to the enemy through that door of disobedience. Satan is always looking for a way into all areas of our lives to take complete control. In the book of 2nd Chronicles we see in chapter 15 that Azariah, the son of Oded prophesied to King Asa of the conditions of God's favour if he and the nations of Judah and Benjamin sought the

Lord God and turn away from the sin of idolatry.

This prophecy came at a time when Israel was void of spiritual leadership. During the time of King Rehoboam the people had abandoned the law of the Lord. *"When the rule of Rehoboam was established and he was strong, he abandoned the law of the Lord, and all Israel with him" (2ⁿᵈ Chronicles 12:1 ESV).* This spiritual departure from God's truth was an error of judgement on King Rehoboam's part and an open door for the nation into state-led idolatry. The spiritual gates were broken down and the people gave themselves over to spiritual deterioration.

In the wake of national apostasy, Israel was invaded by King Shishak of Egypt. God left his people to the marauding group and they were defeated and all but completely destroyed. However it is clear that when King Rehoboam repented God was faithful to have mercy on his nation. *"And when he humbled himself the wrath of the Lord turned from him, so as not to make a complete destruction."(2ⁿᵈ Chronicles 12:12 ESV).* King Rehoboam's contrition was short lived because when he regained his might and strength his pride returned and he continued to do evil in the sight of God.

The decline in spiritual matters continued with King Abijah until King Asa succeeded the throne. The suffering and devastation that followed the reign of King Asa's fore-parents had now reached an apex and restoration and healing was required when God sent Azariah. (3) *"...For a long time Israel was without the true God, and without a teaching priest and without law, (4) but when in their distress they turned to the Lord the God of Israel; and sought him, he was found by them" (2nd Chronicles 15:3-4 ESV).* Generations of national leadership failure had caused the people to err.

Azariah's prophecy illustrated that repentance and the turning away from false worship was the key to access God's favour. King Asa was instructed by God to remove from the land the symbols of the god Asherah that the nations served. He attempted to do so for a time but relented in his spiritual pursuits towards the latter part of his reign.

Previously they had fought the battle with the Ethiopians and won the fight. *"So the Lord defeated the Ethiopians before Asa, and before Judah, and the Ethiopians fled" (2nd Chronicles 14:12 ESV).* God was faithful to help them to secure a victory. The problems Judah and Benjamin were facing were deep-seated generational iniquity. The symbols of worship were erected by the previous generation. It was Asa's mother (or grandmother according to some bible scholars), Maachah who constructed the Asherah poles. *"And also concerning Maachah the mother of Asa the king, he removed her from being queen, because she had made an idol in a grove: and Asa cut down her idol, and stamped it, and burnt it at the brook Kidron." (2 Chronicles 15:16 KJV).*

God now required that her son King Asa enforce a national prohibition against idol worship. As the King he had the power to forbid by law idol worship. Since Maachah's generation did not tear down the altars of sin, the door to a generational passage remained open. The ensuing generation embraced the sins of the fore-parents because their hearts were amenable to the love of false gods. The desire for false worship was instilled deeply in their hearts.

What do we mean by tearing down satanic altars? Tearing or pulling down is not a physical action orchestrated by men but rather, it is stripped away by the Spirit. When we are in agreement with God concerning His Word, the Spirit disposes of our sins. Our hearts are bases that can be used for idol worship. The heart is the seat of our emotions and therefore, we are inclined towards cherishing those things that are dear to us. These treasured objects, individuals or possessions take the glory away from the one and only true God. God is a jealous God and any form of worship to other deities or love, established in the heart to replace His glory is denounced.

4.8   SOCIAL DISORDER

The world has become an unsafe place. Without righteousness and justice, nations struggle with moral and social order. From shore to shore, the global map of what constitutes civil order and nationally secured infrastructures to human socialization has become a blurred landscape. The complex challenges facing the nations have caused mass migration of people seeking to secure a better opportunity in life. The transient metropolis of displaced people has become an international shame. For the Christian, our citizenship is not of this world. We are in the world but we are not of the world. Spiritually, we are ambassadors of the faith and our focus differs from the world order.

With the help of the Most High God, we have an assignment to complete in our lifetime and at times, we long to be home with our Father, the Eternal One. But we are commissioned for an appointed time and until that time, we must face life's uncertainties knowing that God delivers His people from all adverse attacks.

For those called to the "watch tower" of the faith, we cannot turn a blind eye to the distress and plight of those around us. We are commissioned to stand in the gap for our families, communities and nations. We are also commissioned to pray for the peace of Israel. The Word given to the prophet Jeremiah to pluck up, break down, to destroy and to overthrow is given to us to make a difference. *"See, I have this day set thee over the nations and over the kingdoms, to pluck up, and to break down and to destroy and to overthrow, to build and to plant," (Jeremiah 1:10 ASV).*

The enemies of God are warned that His intervention on the behalf of His people will be brutal. We are fighting in a spiritual battle but there are consequences when we interfere with the work of God to bring people out of their captivities. *"God will likewise destroy thee forever; He will take thee up, and pluck thee out of thy tent, and root thee out of the land of the living," (Psalms 52:5 ASV).*

The welfare of souls is of paramount importance to God. Only when we have fought and taken the territories of captivity in spiritual warfare can God commission the work to build and to plant. God declares that He will do the work of rebuilding after the destruction. *"But I will restore you to health and heal your wounds" (Jeremiah 31:17, NIV).* To build and plant on land that is occupied by the enemy is a futile attempt at restoration and healing.

CHAPTER FIVE: THE POWER OF THE WORD

5.1 STRENGTH IN THE WORD

We must pray the Word and believe the Word. God cannot lie. It is impossible for him to lie because His Word is truth. We must believe the Word and understand that it is the power of the Word with the Spirit that secures our blessings.

We are in a fight and so we must be encouraged to stay in the Word and use it to disarm the enemy. The efficacy of the Word renders the opponent incapable of returning fire when we pray. We must keep a worshipful spirit giving God the praise for what He will bring about in our lives. Prayer is a stabilising gird underpinning our faith to help us on the journey of faith. Intercessory praying of the Word is particularly strengthening through the fiery trials of life. At no time must we lose faith and trust in God. Our hope, even though it may seem deferred making us anxious in the pit of our stomach will eventually result in joyfulness. Waiting on God is part of the process of trusting Him and He will not make us ashamed in the face of our enemies. *"Hope deferred makes the heart sick: but when the desire comes, it is a tree of life," (Proverbs 13:12, KJ).*

God will always honour His Word. His exalted Son Jesus is the Word. His reputation to fulfill the Promise to mankind is important to God above all His attributes. His Word is highly esteemed and He has dominion in all situations. *"I will worship toward thy holy temple, and praise thy name for thy lovingkindness and for thy truth: for thou hast magnified thy Word above all thy name," (Psalms 138:2, KJV).*

5.2 CREDIBILITY OF THE WORD

It is said that a man's word is his bond and is a test of his character and credibility. Even sinful man knows that it is important to adhere to his word in order to be proven to be trustworthy. God is the person Truth so He cannot lie. We can depend upon His Word and exercise faith in His Word knowing that it will accomplish in all things. Basically if you cannot honour your word then really you cannot be trusted. Our God is trustworthy in all His ways.

God informs us through the authenticity and credibility of his Word that we can trust Him and depend on Him at all times. The severity of our daily circumstances and our tests are not a dilemma to God. God is not in a predicament concerning the options open to Him relating to peoples, families, communities and nations.

The complex issues to be confronted in times of personal, familial and national crises can be addressed by His Word. John 1:1 attests to the Word as God Himself *"In the beginning was the word, and the Word was with God, and the Word was God,"* ASV. His Word is from the beginning of time, the Alpha. The Word is to the end of time, the Omega. His Word is the Amen and so every fear is settled. Jesus is the anchor of our faith. The Word remains firmly moored in the fiercest of life's storms. The immutable God is the immovable Word that stands secured when everything around our lives become fragmented, unstable, broken and destroyed.

5.3   A Fortified Rock

A rock is a formidable structure that juts out of the land mass or the ocean basin. The Rock of Gibraltar is one such edifice famously known as a tourist attraction. Such a solid structure represents stability having endured variable weather conditions, withstanding stoically over time.

Jesus is the Word sometimes depicted as our Rock of Ages. Our Lord has stood in our place spiritually robust and able to endure every rebuff of the enemy. The enemy is not visible but a spirit. We are flesh and blood and therefore not an equal match against spirits. Jesus is the invisible God and with the eternal host of heaven, they are constantly engaged in fighting on our behalf. *"For we are not fighting against flesh and blood enemies, but against evil rulers and authorities of the unseen world, against mighty powers in this dark world, and against evil spirits in the heavenly places," (Ephesians 6:12).*

We are protected from every attack of the enemy because our Rock is the buffer against every impact. We are no doubt frail, vulnerable and defenseless against demonic agents but in the name of Jesus we are able to overcome the foe. Without Jesus, there would be no protection against the enemy. The fight is not yours or mine, it is God's fight since it has been raging from before the beginning of time. It requires heaven's army, a greater force than the opponent.

5.4   DEPLOYING SPIRITUAL WEAPONS

The enemy fears when the children of God deploy the heavenly resources made available to them through the Word and the Spirit. Our authority to engage in spiritual warfare and fight is in the Word. It is the Word that fights against the adversary. Every time we use the Word, we are engaged in spiritual warfare. It is important to know how to galvanize our efforts using the weapons of our warfare. As prayer agents in the earth, we must be spiritually strong to endure all prevailing conditions that confront us in the stormy seasons of our life. We are pillars in the kingdom fortified through our faith in God. Nothing shall by any means befall us if we remain anchored in Jesus. *"Behold, I have given you authority to tread on serpents and scorpions, and over all the power of the enemy, and nothing shall in anywise hurt you," (Luke 10:19, ASV).*

Now the weapons of our fight are not sensual or earthly which is of the body. Rather, the weapons to deploy in spiritual warfare are powerful through God. *"We use God's mighty weapons, not worldly weapons, to knock down the strongholds of human reasoning and to destroy false arguments," (2 Corinthians 2:10, NLT).* The Word is our weapon that is incredibly accurate to reach and achieve its objective to pull down, root up, and destroy according to Jeremiah 1:10.

5.5 THE FIRE OF GOD

"Is not my Word like fire?" declares the Lord, (Jeremiah 23:29). God makes comparisons to the power of His Word. Firstly, reference is made to the element of fire. The analogy draws parallels with the heat of the Word to melt down and strip away stubborn areas of our personality. Fire has the ability to change a structure when it is burnt. The Word burns into the hearts of men and destroys the works of unrighteousness.

When the Word is fired into the evil stronghold of a situation, it is formidable to tear down and dismantle every opposing strike that comes against its force. If we come up against problems in life, we are to fight back, praying the Word and fasting if we want to overcome.

To get into the flesh by taking matters into our own hands, using the fire power of carnal means is counterproductive tactical warfare in a spiritual fight. We cannot expect to get an answer from God or to see His victorious works over evil when we engage in fleshy spats, even when under provocation. There is no glory for God when we fight by our primal forces. When we are energised by evil and driven to self -directed means, our efforts are futile, and we give the enemy an advantage to regroup and respond with brutal force against us.

5.6   THE HAMMER OF GOD

The hammer of God again is the Word, and it will pulverise to dust all opposing foes. *"Is not my Word like a hammer that breaketh the rock in pieces,"* (Jeremiah 23:29, ASV). Their dust will be scattered by the four winds to the far corners of the earth. The hammer is placed at the root of every evil plant to cut it down. We can have confidence in the Word that it is formidable to destroy the works of darkness in the hearts of men.

CHAPTER SIX: THE WAY FORWARD

If **you** can establish in **your** spirit that without a doubt God is trustworthy and His Word dependable, then **you** can proceed to the next level, which is how to pray effectively. If you do not have faith in the Word then *it is impossible to please God and we can expect nothing from him.   For the just shall live by faith and not by sight.*

6.1   CONFESSIONAL PRAY

Firstly, in order to avoid an attack from the enemy when we pray in a deliverance ministry, we must ask God's forgiveness for sins.

It is important to follow the model of Jesus' prayer "Our Father who art in Heaven."

It is a *seven–fold prayer key*. It is therefore:-

(1) *acknowledges* the One to whom we pray

(2) *recognises* Jesus as the name that is above all names.

(3) *reinforces* the purpose of Jesus' rule and His Sovereign will in the universe.

(4) *recognises* that God is our provider and we need to partake of His Bread daily.

(5) *emphasises* daily confession and forgiveness of our sins towards others.

(6) *acknowledges* that godly protection is needed from the evil one.

(7) *identifies* that all power belongs to the eternal God.

It is imperative that confession is made to God as a daily occurrence. We are fallen creatures and when we respond in prayer to God with a submissive heart there is room for the Spirit to work according to God's will. A spirit of humility and meekness gets the attention of God. The Spirit will reveal the deep and hidden things of the heart that would otherwise be unknown so that we can repent of them. Sins knowingly and unknowingly can be brought to the fore to be dealt with. The Spirit is adept at recovering all hidden malice and unforgiving attitudes that we are expert at keeping secret.

6.2   FORGIVING OTHERS

We pray for forgiveness for those who have hurt us. We also pray against all further activities of the iniquities of our ancestors and fore-parents continuing to blight our lives. These areas of deliverance prayers are intended to cut off the powers of age-long curses and release one from ancestral sins so that our lives and future generations are not blocked by generational curses.

Iniquity is outright rebellion. It is a seditious act of betrayal against God's law. Iniquity is usually rooted deep as to pass to the next generation unless repented of. It is a bond of wickedness.

Sin is usually termed as falling short of what God expects of us. A conscious soul will quickly repent and forsake the sin. It is not an act of rebellion and therefore, is not deeply rooted in one's behavioural pattern. However, if there is no repentance, and the sin is repeated over and over again, in time, it shifts into an iniquitous category because the conscience is excused rather than accused.

Transgressions are entered into when we have committed sin intentionally. It is basically breaking God's law with the mind to do it.

Trespasses are sins that lead one into forbidden territories.

All these categories of sins are done with a greater or lesser measure of intent. God has given unto us free will and therefore when we sin there are spiritually legal implications. Sin is disobeying the divine laws set by God that we are instructed to live by. At no time will God excuse our sins or turn a blind eye to disobedience of His laws. Hence, our fallen nature requires that we continually confess and repent of our sins unto God.

Confession and repentance of sins that we have committed knowingly or unknowingly or those things we have omitted to do are prerequisites to our healing.

CHAPTER SEVEN: PRAYING EFFECTIVELY

7.1 WHAT IS PRAYER?

Praying is the appropriate way to communicate with our Heavenly Father. It is a heavenly channel that is used to beseech God when we have spiritual or earthly needs. We can then ask in faith believing that God will meet our needs according to His mercies. *"Then they cried to the LORD in their trouble, and he saved them from their distress,"* *(Psalms 107:19).*

(6) "But he must ask in faith without any doubting, for the one who doubts is like the surf of the sea, driven and tossed by the wind. (7) For that man ought not to expect that he will receive anything from the Lord, (8) being a double-minded man, unstable in all his ways," *(James 1:6-8).*
Praying takes faith because we do not see God. But we have an assurance in our spirit that He

is near and He hears us. *"Now faith is the substance of things hoped for, the evidence of things not seen," (Hebrews 11:1).* He will grant our needs because He is able to do all things. Our faith is supported in the spirit because it is spirit initiated. Faith is of God, and it keeps working for us even when we are feeling beleaguered and tired in the battle.

Our faith is heartfelt, and we know that when we supplicate before God, we have the Father's love in our innermost being working for our good. It is in that secret place that the dynamic intimacy in prayer takes place. He sups with us bearing us up when all seems to have caved in around us. It is prayer that securely keeps you attached to your eternal hope and trust in God. *"If in this life only we have hope in Christ, we are of all men most miserable," (1 Corinthians 15:19).* When we pray, we are bolstered by the inner strength to keep believing and trusting that God is our provider.

7.2   WHO SHOULD WE PRAY TO?

We pray to God because He is the only one who can forgive us of our sins. Jesus is our advocate and He can intervene before the Father on our behalf. Praying elicits spiritual intervention in matters pertaining to the earthly realm. Without the assistance of heaven, we would be trapped here on earth with a demonic realm sitting over the earth realm. We would be in a spiritual lockdown unable to reach God. The power of our God to subdue the powers of the adversary to get our deliverance and healing is appropriated through prayer. Supplying our needs is important to God. So important is it to God to move on our behalf when we solicit the help of heaven that He sent His only Son to die on the cross for our salvation and deliverance. It is through Jesus that we have access to the throne.

We pray because God alone knows our beginning and our end, and our innermost desires. He is acquainted with our human limitations and strengths. *"For He knows our frame; He remembers that we are dust,"* *(Psalms: 103:14).* He alone knows what your purpose is and the best you can be in your lifetime. David gave thanks to God because He alone knew his frame. The Hebrew word for "frame" is (2) *yetser.* From the OT Septuagint, I find that the Greek meaning for "frame" is *plasma.* This meaning is usually used to bring understanding about the formation of a child or life.

1. (3) Plasma is a cellular-life matter. In the origins of life, plasma is present in the cellular structure of the blood. It is

considered to be the 4th matter in the components of the blood. Plasma plays a crucial, often overlooked role as the fluid that carries the other three components of the blood, namely the white blood cells, red blood cells and platelets. The plasma fluid also contains nutrients, hormones, proteins, salt, water, enzymes, antibodies and clotting agents in the blood to support the body's function.

What my spirit was feeding me concerning the Greek meaning of frame is that God, according to Psalms 103:14 knows our make up. He is familiar with our cellular formation in the origins of our life. He knows every faulty gene and the weaknesses of our "DNA" structure. Every composite of our being, He has acquainted Himself with in the eternities long before we became tangible created matter. How marvelous is that? Our entire being including our ethereal substance and matter He has prior knowledge of. We were curiously worked on in our unborn state. *"My frame was not hidden from you, when I was being made in secret, intricately woven in the depths of the earth,"* *(Psalms 139:15).*

All that we need in our lifetime for our peace and to fulfill our purpose is known to God.

There is nothing about you that God is not familiar with. Even before you pray, he knows what your request will be. From before the foundation of the world, He saw you making that request, and He had already from then determined how to meet that need. The Spirit of God bears us up when we pray, and He has eternal knowledge about you that is not revealed to you as yet. The Spirit prepares us for those challenges that are to be time-released into our lives long before they become active.

We just have to go through the process of learning to trust God. He gets the glory when our needs are met, and we come through the battle stronger for the experience. Our testimonies speak of His awesome power to meet our requests no matter how trivial it may seem to others or embarrassing to you. There is nothing He cannot do for His obedient children. So why worry when everything is cupped in the hands of God. He constantly looks down at you in the cup of His hands. *"Your hands have made me and fashioned me: give me understanding" (Psalms 119:73).*

7.3   WHY SHOULD WE PRAY?

Firstly, we are biblically instructed to pray without ceasing. We pray because we need the help of God. The spiritual journey is met with hostility because the warfare we are in is against an evil spiritual realm opposed to the things of God. Those who declare through His Word to be Christians will inadvertently become a target. The fight has never been ours. *"For we wrestle not against flesh and blood, but against principalities, against powers, against the rulers of the darkness of this world, against spiritual wickedness in high places,"* (Ephesians 6:12). Our Lord is sovereign in our battles. Ensure that you are fighting on the Lord's side. For the rule of His kingdom is justice and righteousness. The weapons we use in this fight are not fleshy ones but the weapons of our warfare are mighty through God demolishing strongholds, *"For the weapons of our warfare are not of the flesh but have divine power to destroy strongholds." (2 Corinthians 10:4-5 ESV).*

All that we do for God must be done with a true heart. You cannot fast and pray to God and then rise up to fight with the fists of wickedness. God is a being of love. He is compassionate and righteous and all His ways are just. If we say that we are Christians, and we live according to the Word of God then our actions must align with God's Word. Our conduct should befit the exemplary character of Jesus our Lord. If we are energized to destroy life and others with a different viewpoint then we need to question of what kingdom we belong.

7.4 WHY ENGAGE IN SPIRITUAL WARFARE?

There are those who believe that once you are saved you are delivered. If you wish to entertain such thinking then by all means feel free to do so. The Word tells us to increase in the knowledge of God. *"...asking that you may be filled with the knowledge of his will in all spiritual wisdom and understanding, so as to walk in a manner worthy of the Lord, fully pleasing to him, bearing fruit in every good work and increasing in the knowledge of God."* *(Colossians 1:9-10 ESV).*

When we are newly saved it is just the start of an incredible journey with Jesus. There is so much to discover along the way that it requires fervency and faith in God. There remain many areas of one's life that require healing and deliverance. However, it is by far a journey not intended for those who are swift to the finishing line but for those who will persevere to the end not shirking from their responsibilities.

There was a time when Christians were able to pray in a less than strategic manner as we have been accustomed to do. The fight has changed and it is becoming increasingly difficult for people to remain steadfast in the faith. What has changed? I believe we have reached an impasse in the body of Christ. It has become impossible for Christians to carry on customarily. As in any warfare, there are times when the fight is more intense. Our fight is not in isolation but we are a unit working against the machinations of a spiritually artful set up of evil. The mastermind behind the covert operations of the evil realm has but a short time to make an impact on the church.

The Apostle Paul reminded the church at Ephesus that the fight of those in the Lord Jesus was against a strategically ingenious and complex linear force of evil. It is a set up of immense power forcefully strong to achieve a desired end. As human beings, without heavenly assistance, we are not equally matched against this spiritual force. Their works are hidden and it takes the power of the cross to reveal and disrupt their operations. *"Finally, be strong in the Lord and in the strength of his might. (11) Put on the whole armour of God, that ye may be able to stand against the wiles of the devil. (12) For our wrestling is not against flesh and blood, but against the powers, against the world rulers of this darkness, against the spiritual hosts of wickedness in the heavenly places," (Ephesians 6: 11-12, ASV).*

We all have to step up to a greater dimension of spiritual fighting. To unseat the demon occupying areas of your life requires a greater level of praying in the Spirit. If you do the same thing over and over again, you will get the same results each time. A new approach is required for these times through spiritual warfare. It just means an intense combative approach to praying because we are determined not to allow the enemy to succeed against us. Use the Word to pound his gates and destroy his powerbase. His stranglehold on the people of God is restrictive and designed to immobilise them with his fear tactics. *"God has not given us the spirit of fear but of power, and of love and of a sound mind,"* (2 Timothy 1:7 KJV).

7.5   HOW DO WE FIGHT?

We fight by upholding the righteousness of God. To do anything else is to get into the flesh, and we will be 'picked off' by the enemy. Satan knows when we have sinned or fallen which gives him the opportunity to accuse us before God. If we are lawbreakers and we have not asked forgiveness and repented, Satan has the legal right to torment us. If we do not pray and use the Word to get out of our sins, we remain guilty before God. How often Christians leave themselves open to the enemy having a foothold in their lives because they will not forsake sin and turn away from it penitently. *"But if we confess our sins to him, he is faithful and just to forgive us our sins and to cleanse us from all wickedness," (1 John 1:19).*

Many people are afraid to fully engage in the fight for the territories that God has given them. Consequently, many areas of their lives are blocked, unproductive and blighted by demonic occupation. The majority of Christians live spiritually impoverished lives. They do not know how to make the Word work for them. They are constantly depending on others to pray for them. Learn to do it for yourself and stop being so needy. Your behaviour contradicts the power of the Word.

God told His people that when they possessed the land given to them, they must drive out the inhabitants little by little. Now we know that Israel did the opposite. They did not tear down the altars of strange gods nor did they fully occupy the territory. They inter-married with the heathens and settled to co-exist with the enemy. It was only a matter of time before their failure to obey God's instructions would bear fruits.

Disobedience to God gives access to the enemy and as a result, we suffer because of our disobedience and ignorance. It is important to understand this one truth concerning spiritual warfare. We are all engaged in the fight albeit at different levels of operation. Those who say that they do not want to engage in spiritual warfare because of fear of unsettling their lives speak out of error.

Every time we use the Word against the activities of the enemy, we are engaged in spiritual warfare. It is a myth to think that spiritual warfare is something being done by Christians to elicit the wrath of Satan because they are entering unnecessarily into forbidden spiritual territories. The term "spiritual warfare" may conjure up thoughts of unnecessary territorial fights with Satan. No! It is simply using the Word with authority. It is learning to be more proactive rather than reactive to your life situations.

Spiritual warfare provides deep inner cleansing of the entities of life. If we do not thoroughly cleanse our life we will live in fear and torment over issues that could be obliterated by deliverance prayer. We must be proactive in spending time securing the territories of our lives that God has entrusted us to. The children of Israel made that mistake and neglected to discharge the enemies from the land God gave to them and so they had to suffer the consequences.

We become accustom to living with our problems rather than seek to be rid of them. When Jesus passed by the colonnades with the five porches where the sick, crippled and diseased lay by the pool of Bethesda, he met a man who was crippled for thirty-eight years.

Jesus knowing that it was a chronic case asked the man if he wanted to be made whole. Why would Jesus ask him that question? I believe that faith plays a key role in our healing and on many occasions Jesus remarked on the faith of the seeker.

Jesus wanted the man to confess his faith by declaring that he desired to be healed. He would make attempts to get into the churning water but he was not quick enough off the mark to enter into the pool. *"After this there was a feast of the Jews, and Jesus went up to Jerusalem. Now there is in Jerusalem by the Sheep Gate a pool, which is called in Hebrew, Bethesda, having five porches. In these lay a great multitude of sick people, blind, lame, paralyzed, waiting for the moving of the water. For an angel went down at a certain time into the pool and stirred up the water; then whoever stepped in first, after the stirring of the water, was made well of whatever disease he had. Now a certain man was there who had an infirmity thirty-eight years. When Jesus saw him lying there, and knew that he already had been in that condition a long time, He said to him, "Do you want to be made well?" The sick man answered Him, "Sir, I have no man to put me into the pool when the water is stirred up; but while I am coming, another steps down before me." Jesus said to him, "Rise, take up your bed and walk." And immediately the man was made well, took up his bed, and walked. And that day was the Sabbath. (John 5:1-9)*

If we desire to be made whole we must do something to get the attention of Jesus. That principle still applies to us today.

The fight is not with you remember! It is the Word that fights the enemy. All you have to do is use the Word with authority in Jesus' name. Whenever you use the Word in your situation you are engaged in a spiritual war because the enemy comes against the Word. Satan does not want the people of God to be delivered and enjoy the rest and peace to the extent that we can in our temporal lives. Hence, those who commit to extricating the enemy from their land by using the power of the Word with greater authority will initially come under attack. Spiritual warfare is using the Word with greater authority by being combative and resilient. For the kingdom comes under attack but those who are spiritually violent will take it by force. It is the Word that fights the enemy.

The greater the aggression towards you as you tear down the altars and high places in your life, family, community or nation is the greater the level of spiritual authority God has given to you. Some people may lose everything for their call whilst the majority will not. The level of spiritual authority God has given me required so much of me because to whom much is given much is required. What I had to endure is not what the majority would have to go through. To step out by faith and make a difference gets the attention of the enemy. Satan takes note when one is marked out by God to advance the cause of His kingdom of righteousness.

The strategy of the enemy is to distress those who are on the frontline of the warfare with constant attacks. Sometimes, a person is engaged in one fight after the other. Do not be weary in well doing because God is in control of all things. The resistance will come from those who need your prayer most. Spiritual interference is intended to impede the breakthrough that people so desperately need. The frontline workers are not the intended targets. So fiercely fought is the spiritual war that close family relationships can be broken as you endeavour to stand in the gap. You are nonetheless encouraged to obey God rather than man.

Tough love requires that you fight with the spiritual objective in view as opposed to the immediate gratifications the people desire. The relationship with people is not as important as your relationship with God. Jesus encountered the same fierce resistance when the people were used by Satan to cry "crucify him." His people rejected Him and today many are still in spiritual darkness as to who He is and His awesome power to deliver them out of their spiritual bondage. It is those closest to you who the enemy will use to disorganise and disrupt your prayer effort. They are the ones crying "crucify him."

The hostility towards you is a provocation to intimidate you to remain in a defensive position. It is the Spirit that prompts you to dispense with fear and to boldly engage in a higher level of authority and responsibility in the fight for your marriage, families, communities and nations. The level God has called you to serve at, he will provide the necessary spiritual protection for you to operate at that level. You must know where God has called you to serve and stay in your territory. If God has not called you to go to the nations then do not take it upon yourself to go- that will prove to be a grave mistake.

Luke 4 illustrates how a person can come under demonic occupation so that all areas of his/her life are bound. This case required the intervention of Jesus and it was recorded for His glory. We see how Jesus has authority over all demonic strongholds.

It matters not how dire and hopeless your case may seem to others. Mary Magdalene would have been in a pitiable condition to be held captive under a seven-fold demonic stranglehold. She was under the perfect control of evil, and it took the Saviour of the people to show up and command an end to the demonic reign.

These kinds of spirits are embedded deeply in the personality of the victim. A greater level of spiritual authority is required to disperse and route them out of their "familiar" residence. When people who have been under such levels of attack have recovered from their bondage, they are the best advocates of Jesus' power to heal. If people have never been where Mary Magdalene was, righteous in their own eyes, they have no need to show an attitude of thankfulness to God. Mary Magdalene knew what Jesus' ministry meant to her. She was eternally grateful to be released from such a strong captivity of evil. She was an ardent witness and follower of Jesus to the end of His earthly life.

7.6   BINDING THE STRONGMAN

"For who is powerful enough to enter the house of a strong man like Satan and plunder his goods? Only someone even stronger-- someone who could tie him up and then plunder his house," (Matthew 12:29, NLT).

The strongman in this scripture is revealed as Satan. He is behind problems in the lives of people, communities, governments and nations. It is Jesus who has been given the authority by God to forbid Satan's activities over all entities of life. It takes a greater power to subdue his power.   That power has been given to the people of God to bind the spirit behind the problem and to loose healing and deliverance in the name of Jesus. *"I will give you the keys of the kingdom of heaven; whatever you bind on earth will be bound in heaven, and whatever you loose on earth will be loosed in heaven,"* *(Matthew 16:19)* NIV.

Deliverance prayer is embarking on a deep cleaning of your spiritual house. Your house is the heart or temple of the presence of God. *"Know ye not that ye are a temple of God, and that the Spirit of God dwelleth in you?"* *(1 Corinthians 3:16)* KJV.   We carry so much bondage through our lifetime not knowing how to rid ourselves of them. Because of the lack of knowledge concerning the strategies to use against the opponent, we are disadvantaged in the fight.

When you bind and cast out the strongmen ruling areas of your life you leave your house swept and emptied out of their presence. *(24)* *"When an impure spirit comes out of a person, it goes through arid places seeking rest and does not find it. Then it says, 'I will return to the house I left.' (25) When it arrives, it finds the house swept clean and put in order." (26) Then it goes and takes seven other spirits more wicked than itself, and they go in and live there.*

And the final condition of that person is worse than the first," (Luke 11:24-26) NIV. Basically, they leave to find another residence since spirits can only operate through host bodies.

When they wander in dry places and they cannot find a host body, they will seek to return to a familiar ground. If the place is swept and cleaned but still empty, it means that you have not taken the time to fill up with the Word and prayer. An empty house is a sign to an illegal lodger that no one is home so he takes over the place inviting seven friends to come in and share the residence. It is therefore important to keep your house full of the presence of the Lord after you have emptied out the spirits through undergoing deliverance prayer.

We keep our house occupied by reading the Word and praying in the Spirit, filling up the emptied territory. We can combine these with singing psalms, meditating in the presence of the Lord and praising God. These are ways we must frequently employ in order to dwell in the atmosphere of His Presence. If you neglect to do these and revert to your indisciplined prayer life, over time you will cause the spirits you have cast out to return. The Word tells us that they enter again seven-fold stronger and your state will be worse than before. The numeral seven is completion or substantial. Therefore, the spirits will come back strengthened as a complete and substantial reoccupation. The state of that person will be worse than before they had the spiritual cleansing.

7.7   WHEN TO PRAY

There are no set times to pray unless you have allotted time accordingly through a prayer strategy or plan. However, we must always permit the Holy Spirit to direct us and lead us into prayer. It is the Holy Spirit who ushers us into the presence of God. Under His prompting, we sometimes feel a burden or longing to be in the presence of our Father. Other times, one may just feel ecstatic joy to praise and worship God. Meditative, holy quietness before God are also precious moments initiated by the Spirit. Just follow the leading of the Spirit.

Our lifestyle should be one of continually praying, therefore, the formality of kneeling is not a pre-requisite to presenting ourselves to God. Communicating in prayer is just one aspect of our relationship with God. We can approach Him as and when we feel a need to as prompted by the Spirit. Our praises and thanksgiving are offerings unto God as is reading and praying the Word. Equally, we may wish to pray alone, in pairs or as a group offering unto God. The place to pray is limitless. Some people use the time in an airplane to pray into the atmosphere. Others pray and walk taking territories. Others go to the mountains to be alone with God. Your pray closet needs not be the prayer shawl but anywhere you choose to be with your God. For some they have no choice, they may be incarcerated like Joseph. Whenever you are prompted to pray, remember God is with you because He is everywhere in His universe.

Prayer is not only vocalized but one can meditate as mentioned earlier or pray without the expression of words. Hannah was the wife of Elkanah, a serving priest. She was barren and longed for her womb to be opened by God. In her deep anguish, she prayed to the LORD, weeping bitterly in the temple in the presence of the high priest Eli, (1Samuel 1:10). Eli was old in age and his spiritual efficacy was undesirable before God. He mistook Hannah for being drunken and rebuked her. Out of her grieving spirit she uttered "No my lord. I am not drunk but a woman burdened in spirit." Eli's natural eyes were dim, and it is safe to say that his natural state paralleled the spiritual state.

When there are no words, and we are broken and silent, we are understood by the Spirit who makes sense of what we are conveying even through our tears. Our emotional state can be a determining factor of when we pray. When one is troubled or bowed low in spirit, there is usually a deep inner need to go before the throne of God. The psalmist David declared that God is the lifter up of our heads.

There are times we just exclaim "Oh God!" or shout "Oh Jesus help me!" These moments may be times of emergency when we can only call out of our desperate situation. Be assured, God hears you and in those times heavenly assistance is made available.

7.8   HOW TO PRAY

I use the *7-FOLD PRAYER PLAN* when necessary to procure deliverance and healing. It works for me, and it is my own method for intercessory praying. It is simple and effective, and I would recommend it to those who desire to pray effectively. It is not intended to be a prescriptive approach to prayer. We must always rely upon the Holy Spirit to direct us into prayer. There are different ways to seek the help of God, and it is what works best for you that will be appropriate. The most important thing in praying is that your heart is clean before God. Confess sins that are known and unknown and forgive your enemies. These two actions are the prerequisite to hearing from God.

Some people combine praying with fasting. This is an effective approach but must be done with wisdom. One must seek advice if they are on medication or not accustomed to fasting. Determine the reason why you are fasting, the time allocated to the fast and commit that to God reverently and prayerfully.

The Word tells us to pray according to the Scripture that informs us. As the warfare intensifies, we need to be fully armed with effective weapons. Therefore, we are commanded to employ the weapons of the Word because they are not carnal but mighty through God to the pulling down of the strongholds of Satan. We come in agreement with the Word about ourselves. If God is saying that you are unclean before him then agree with Him and cleanse yourself. As we approach the throne of God, we humbly submit to His chastening in the Word. We will see ourselves as we look upon our Saviour in the mirror of the Word. There can be no pretence or show but willingly, we confess who we are. We must believe the Word and declare it in our situation.

7.9   PRAYING FROM THE HEART

Can a man know the errors of his ways? It is an emphatic "no!" We cannot truly understand or perceive the depth of our fallen nature. It is the Spirit who reveals the true state of the heart. It is the Spirit who knows our thoughts, intents and motives.   (1) To illustrate the profound knowledge of the Holy Spirit, bible scholars have used the Hebrew word "chaaqar." It brings understanding in Psalm 139:1, *"O LORD, you have searched me and known me!"* David understood that the Lord accurately analyses the hidden and secret things conceived and birthed out of him. For out of our mouths decant the issues of the heart. *"And he who searches our hearts knows the mind of the Spirit, because the Spirit intercedes for God's people in accordance with the will of God,"* (Romans 8:27).

"The spirit of man is the lamp of the LORD, searching all his innermost parts,"
(Proverbs 20:27). Here again, reference is made to the role of the Holy Spirit in shedding light in the dark regions of the soul. Deep in the birth chamber where we were curiously fashioned our God had perceptive wisdom concerning our being even before that time. "The term "curiously wrought" is the Hebrew *"raqam"* meaning *"embroidered," or "did*

needlework." To undertake tapestry work is a tedious, painstakingly meticulous task. It requires paying attention to details because of the intricate skills required.

God took time over our matter and substance deeply positioned in the womb. He watched over us and left nothing to chance. How marvellous is His loving kindness towards the children of man. He knows our frame and the substance of who we are.

God is the Ancient of Days and His knowledge of all things precedes time and age. With this understanding, we can come boldly before Him and unburden at His feet. When we pray, He understands our pains and frustrations even when we cannot fully explain our feelings. In fact, God felt your pain and saw your situation before time came into existence. How wonderful is the thought that we were in the mind of God long before we came into being.

The Spirit pleads on our behalf as we groan longingly for our innermost needs to be met. *"And the Holy Spirit helps us in our weakness. For example, we do not know what to pray and how to pray. But the Holy Spirit prays for us with groanings that cannot be expressed in words," (Romans 8:26).* This is just such a powerful verse of scripture because there is nothing more intensely satisfying in the spirit than when we are called away from the cares of this life for an audience before The Presence.

It is there, in those moments of meaningful and blissful intimacy that deep levels of utterance, invoked by the Spirit takes place. We are fragile and weighed down at times, cumbered with a load of life's cares but we can take it to our Heavenly Father and leave it there.

7.10   PRAYING GOD'S WILL

The Word instructs us to pray for others including world and governmental leaders. *"First of all, then, I urge that supplications, prayers, intercessions, and thanksgivings be made for all people, [2] for kings and all who are in high positions, that we may lead a peaceful and quiet life, godly and dignified in every way. [3] This is good, and it is pleasing in the sight of God our Savior, [4] who desires all people to be saved and to come to the knowledge of the truth"* (1Timothy 2:1-4).

This is so important particularly in these pressuring times when the world system is being engineered to curtail our civil liberties. People's movement, and the relatively free social order of life we have known is now being interfered with and manipulated at a strategic global level. It is scriptural and will cause untold misery to human existence ushering in the rapture of the saints. Albeit, not before the people of God experience a time of refreshing in the Spirit. We are about to see a season of exceptional glorious outpouring of healing and reconciliation to the things of God. That time has come!

We are also to pray for the peace of Israel. *"Pray for the peace of Jerusalem! 'May they be secure who love you!'" (Psalms 122:6).* In Genesis 12:3, it records, that those who bless Israel will be blessed by God, and those who curse Israel will be cursed by God.

Israel has played a significant role in the civilization of the nations. Furthermore, they are God's chosen people. They were favoured as the ancestral lineage for our Lord Jesus. Jesus came to bring salvation to the world because God loves everyone and it is His desire that we all come to repentance for the saving of our souls. Jesus is chosen for man's redemption from the foundation of the world.

The same spirit that was around to block the ministry of Jesus is wreaking havoc in Christian communities around the globe. The spirit that hates Jesus caused Herod to seek out the baby Jesus for His demise. It further launched itself against the prophets and apostles who bore witness of the Christ, the Anointed One.

As we draw nearer to the rapture of the saints, it is evident that the assault against Christians has increased leading to atrocities in our world. The spiritual fight has intensified, and we are being drawn into aggressive combative spiritual warfare. Those who love Jesus will find themselves fighting more intensely than ever before to keep the territories of their faith. Satan is the principal demon at work wreaking havoc in the nations to avert the end time will of God for the nations. *"Satan, who is the god of this world, has blinded the minds of those who don't believe. They are unable to see the glorious light of the Good News. They don't understand this message about the glory of Christ, who is the exact likeness of God, (2ⁿᵈ Corinthians 4:4)* NLT.

Again, we see in the Epistle of Paul to the small new Christian community of Thessalonica that they are encouraged to pray continually for each other. *(16) Rejoice always; (17) pray without ceasing; (18) in everything give thanks; for this is God's will for you in Christ Jesus (1 Thessalonians 5:16-18).* Clearly, praying is an integral element of our walk with God. It has been said that *"seven days without prayer makes one weak."*

It is imperative that we pray the will of the Father for our lives, families, communities and nations that the evil reign over these atmospheres are shaken to their core. Satan has raised his ugly head in the nations and the evil ushered in upon the small Christian communities is not of God. We are instructed by the apostle Paul to *"pray always with all prayer and supplication in the Spirit, and watching thereunto with all perseverance and supplication for all saints"* (Ephesians 6:8). Christian communities living under brutal regimes where they are oppressed and unable to freely engage in worship to God need the prayers of those in the Western nations who are not experiencing undue restriction or persecution in their worship.

The Spirit of God knows the mind of God. What is in the mind of God concerning us can only be revealed through the Spirit of God. When we pray in the Spirit we allow the Spirit to intercede on our behalf before the Father. What is in the mind of God is then made known to us so that we can pray it into our lives in the will of God.

The spirit of revelation is one of the characteristics embodied in the personhood of the Spirit. He will reveal all things to us because He speaks what is in the mind of God. God desires that we be informed about what we are up against. *"However when he, the Spirit of truth, has come, he will guide you into all truth, for he will not speak from himself; but whatever he hears, he will speak. He will declare to you things that are coming" (John 16:13, World English Bible).*

Pray in different ways as the Spirit directs. That could be confessional, meditative, intercessory etc. Pray in the Spirit to know the will of God for our lives as revealed by the Father. *"In the same way, the Spirit helps us in our weakness. We do not know what we ought to pray for, but the Spirit himself intercedes for us through wordless groans" (Romans 8:26, NIV).*

It is prayer that will subdue the powers of evil upon the nations. God has not turned a blind eye to the suffering of His people. Biblically, we see great favour bestowed on the children of Israel. The same God will protect and favour Zion in these times. His power of deliverance will be evident as He turns the hearts of the people to His will.

7.11   PRAYING IN THE SPIRIT

Praying in the Spirit is a compelling and powerful approach to demolishing the works of evil. The Word of God with the Spirit is forcibly potent to shift nations and people into the obedience of Christ Jesus who is Head over all creation.

When the Spirit bears up our spirit in the Word, great things are accomplished in the realms beyond our human understanding. Demonic forces are uprooted from territories and routed out seven different ways when God's appointed time is dawned. It is a perfect dispersion as the enemies of God are scattered and their operations are paralysed and demolished.

Jesus is depicted as the "Restorer of the Breach" in Isaiah 58.   He restores the uninhabitable places to peaceable dwellings when the powers of oppression and the bonds of evil are broken through prayer and fasting. *"The weapons we fight with are not the weapons of the world. On the contrary, they have divine power to demolish strongholds,"* *(2nd Corinthians 10:4, NIV).* We are armed with powerful weaponry for a spiritual fight. When we use what is at our disposal as given to us through Jesus our Lord, we are able to overcome all works of evil by the power of the cross.

7.12 FOUNDATIONAL PRAYING

Self-discipline cannot eradicate the rooted problems in your life. Take the time to pray starting with (1) breaking ties with what you know of your parents' life from time of conception, (2) any problems resulting in rejection in the womb and an inability to bond with significant caregivers (3) problems in your early pre-school years; (4) your early and primary school years, (5) adolescence years, (6) early adulthood years and (7) adulthood and your entire life cycle. You must desire Jesus to be Lord of your whole life. Allow the Spirit to recall the unpleasant memories of your past and break the powers that have held you in those areas. This is important because you must deal with the fragmented self. It is time to face your fears and permit the Spirit to heal you and put you back together again. Forgive and move on with the rest of your life.

Since we are faulty in our human make up we need to ensure that we are building our lives on the sure foundation of the Word. If our foundations are broken and destroyed how will we endure the stormy seasons of life? We will experience constant setbacks and failure at every juncture of life because the same mistakes are made.

Your coping skills and how you approach life becomes a negative pattern of behaviour. You must be totally honest so that all your inner most thoughts, actions, feelings and desires are yielded from the dark recesses of the mind and confessed to your Father in heaven. When we are ashamed of past sins, hurt by others or rejected we are prone to *'shut down'* and repress the pain and experiences. However the true state of the heart is revealed when life triggers emit a flow of emotional lava from the inner turmoil. The Holy Spirit is the revealer of the hidden matters of the mind. We are inclined towards forgetting the unpleasant things and live in denial. But if we permit Him to search our hearts he will bring release from captivity.

7.13 TERRITORIAL WATCH

Always be vigilant over the areas God has given you authority to watch and pray.
These territories are your life, your family, your marriage, your ministry, your business and finances etc. The list goes on. God has placed others in the gwatchtower over churches, communities, and nations. You will know where the burden of your remit lies. *"I will take*

my stand at my watch post and station myself on the tower, and look out to see what he will say to me, and what I will answer concerning my complaint." *(Habakkuk 2:1) ESV.* It is good to have a questioning spirit concerning the things of God. With a seeking, discerning spirit do not just pray but listen, receive when He speaks and enquire for more clarification.

When praying over territories be aware that you are dealing with strong spirits of witchcraft. They manipulate and control areas and are reluctant to give them up once they have secured the area. Pray against any backlash from such tenacious grip of evil. Stay within the remit of territorial warfare that God has given to you until you have conquered those areas and advance yet further as the Spirit permits.

CHAPTER EIGHT: THE 7-FOLD PRAYER PLAN

P lease use the guide primarily as a prompt and be led of the Spirit. You will know when you are covering ground as the Spirit gives you a witness in your spirit.

KEY 1. CONFESSIONS AND REPENTANCE

I bring myself in confession and repentance. I acknowledge that I am a sinner saved by grace. There is no good in me that I should come before you the eternal God. Confess sins and ask Forgiveness *"and forgive us our sins, as we have forgiven those who have sinned against us," (Matthew 6:12)* ISV.

Be quick to forgive your enemies and release them to God because they are not worthy of your time. Negative preoccupation with your enemies is futile expenditure of an invaluable commodity such as time.

KEY 2: THY WILL BE DONE

Thank you Father for being my God. Thank you for your mercies towards me. Thank Him that through the Word made flesh in Jesus you can come boldly to the cross. It is in the name of Jesus that we obtain the victory. Galatians 3: 13

Thank Him for His purpose towards mankind in the earth and that His Will is done under the Headship of our Lord Jesus.

KEY 3: PREPARE FOR BATTLE

Always put on the full armour of God when you are going into warfare prayer. Just say 'I now cover myself with the full armour of God's protection according to Ephesians 6'. *(11)"Put on the whole armour of God, that ye may be able to stand against the wiles of the devil. (12) For our wrestling is not against flesh and blood, but against the principalities, against the powers, against the world rulers of this darkness, against the spiritual hosts of wickedness in the heavenly places (13) Wherefore take up the whole armour of God, that ye may be able to withstand in the evil day, and, having done all, to stand. (14) Stand therefore, having girded your loins with truth and having put on the breastplate of righteousness, (15) and having shod your feet with the preparation of the gospel of peace; (16) withal taking up the shield of faith, wherewith ye shall be able to quench all the fiery darts of the evil one. (17) And take the helmet of salvation, and the sword of the Spirit which is the Word of God: (18) with all prayer and supplication praying at all seasons in the Spirit ..." (Ephesians 6:11-18) ASV.*

Put on each element of protection whilst covering your family also. Sometimes to conserve time I just personalise verse 11.

KEY 4: BREAKING GENERATIONAL COVENANTS

In this section, you would need to spend time renouncing all covenants you have entered into knowingly or unknowingly. These covenants will include the sins of your father's house and your mother's house. I also include the sins of my spiritual parents' houses. We do not need to know what their sins were because we could not know anyway. The principle is merely to disconnect with their iniquities and ask God to forgive them, thus ending the generational passage of covenants. Break all covenants and ties in the spirit realm and release those who have hurt you, used and abused you.

Ask forgiveness for all your trespasses, sins, iniquities and transgressions you committed. In the initial stages of going through deliverance, you will need to ask forgiveness for sins committed throughout your lifetime. Again, you may not know of some or do not remember but the Spirit can bring things back to your remembrance. The idea is to say, "I confess my sins, the sins of my fore-parents that we have entered into knowingly or unknowingly. I ask forgiveness on behalf of my father's house and my mother's house going back to Adam and Eve. I also ask forgiveness on behalf of my spiritual fathers' houses and spiritual mothers' houses. I take authority in the name of Jesus and command release from legal ties," *(here you can name the spiritual ties familiar to your family).* Spiritual ties can be identified as recurring sins or problems manifesting in the family across generations.

Below I set out some examples of praying the Word, making declarations and employing the weapons of the Word to destroy the areas of your life that require deliverance. Each example should not be just read as it is but used to thoroughly cleanse the foundations of your familial, marital, relational, ministerial, financial realms and other areas of your life. Praying deliverance prayers is hard work and time-consuming. It requires dedication as the Spirit reveals what you should pray.

This plan is only intended as a guide and is by no means comprehensive. To be effective in deliverance ministration you must be thorough in your prayer as you wait on the Spirit to direct you.

KEY 5:   RENOUNCING PRAYER

As Part of Key 4 to break generational covenants, it is imperative to renounce those things or deeds entered into knowingly or unknowingly. The definition given to the word "renounce" according to the *Cambridge Dictionary* is:- *"To say formally or publicly that you no longer own, support, believe in, or have a connection with something."* Hence, why it is important to decree or declare a thing by vocalising loudly into the atmosphere. It is to release what is being said openly.

The apostle Paul instructed the church at Corinth, *"But have renounced the hidden things of dishonesty, not walking in craftiness, nor handling the word of God deceitfully; but by manifestation of the truth commending ourselves to every man's conscience in the sight of God,"* (2 Corinthians 4:2, KJV). When we renounce the secrets of our hearts, the enemy no longer has power over you. His aim is to keep you silent because it is an unclean spirit at work when we are mute. Have you ever encountered a spiritual attack and you try to shout out "Jesus" and you feel as though you are being muzzled? It is an unclean spirit gagging you.

When engaging in renouncing prayers, I would advise fasting for at least 1 day as a level of extra protection. One must not engage in renouncing prayers unless they are saved. If the prayer is being done collectively then it is wise for the facilitator of the group to identify those who are not born again and ask them not to say these prayers. Once they have confessed Jesus as Lord and accepted Him as their Saviour, take them through the sinner's prayer. Only then can they begin to relinquish any legal entities they have entered into pertaining to their own spiritual cleansing. Again, I stress it must be a basic level of renouncing the hidden works of darkness from their lives.

Only those who believe they have the spiritual authority should enter into advanced renunciation of spiritual territories. It is the Spirit of God who urges and qualifies one for advancement in any area of the deliverance ministry. It is not His will that we be destroyed because of zeal and spiritual ignorance, but that the knowledge of God is sought to avoid unnecessary attacks from the enemy.

Steps to take prior to engaging in renouncing prayer:

- *Ensure that you are saved by being born again.*
  That is according to the 3-fold acceptance of faith:-
  (1) Believing that Jesus is the Son of God.
  (2) That Jesus died for your sins
  (3) That Jesus is able to forgive you of your sins. On the confession of your faith, you are born again. *"...that if you confess with your mouth Jesus as Lord, and believe in your heart that God raised Him from the dead, you will be saved;"* (Romans 10:9 ESV)

- *Do any renouncing prayer with a deliverance minister* if you are newly saved or not familiar with this type of ministry. For those in the categories above please do your prayer pertaining to *personal deliverance*. Do not attempt to renounce in advanced areas of the deliverance ministry.

- It is a good practice to *do a 1-day fast prior to doing the renouncing prayers*. It is extra covering and also starts the process of weakening and the breaking down of the stubborn areas before the prayer commences.

- *Cover yourself and your family* by putting on the complete armour of God according to Ephesians 6:12. Do not leave off any element of the covering.

- *Make confession* of known or unknown sins.

- *Forgive your enemies* and release them to God.

- *Say the renouncing prayer aloud* to transform the atmosphere.

KEY 6: MAINTAINING YOUR HEALING

Once you embark on praying in this manner there can be no reverting to your usual prayer life. It has to become a way of life.

You must increase in the reading of the Word. These chapters will not include the periods of study time spent in the Word. The idea is not to be religious but rather to permit the Spirit to direct your time of prayer and consecration as a lifestyle. When praying, you will know when you have had a victory because you will begin to praise God spontaneously with a witness in your spirit.

KEY 7:   READING ALOUD

After you have engaged in deliverance praying always conclude the session by reading aloud a number of scriptures and praying in the Spirit. Many people read the scriptures silently. The power of the Word is exercised when it penetrates the atmosphere. It must be spoken and released to accomplish its work. We must engage in territorial warfare and that is decreeing the Word to destroy, tear down, and pull up the constructions and plantings of evil. The forcibly penetrating Word of God when sent forth succeeds in the things of God.

These simple disciplines will clear your spiritual atmosphere and disperse any heaviness you may be feeling as your body will actually feel the effects of a spiritual fight. It is therefore important that you know that the Word will clear your atmosphere in order to feel refreshed and alert after a session of deliverance praying.

SCRIPTURES DECLARATIONS ACTIONS

"God has not given us the spirit of fear but of power and of love and a sound mind" (2 Timothy 1:7).

"See, I have this day set thee over the nations and over the kingdoms, to root out, and to pull down, and to destroy, and to throw down, to build, and to plant," (Jeremiah 1:10)

Psalms 107:20: "He sent his word and he healed them and delivered them from destruction."

I declare according to
2 Timothy 1:7 that the spirit of fear is not my portion. I am a servant of the Most High God and I stand in the authority of the Word. I employ the Word according to Jeremiah 1:10 to root up, pull down and destroy etc.
I now decree healing according to Psalms 107:20.
I am more than a conqueror and able to accomplish all in the name of Jesus.

Use the fire of the Word or the hammer of the Word to destroy areas of your life. e.g.

(1) "In the name of Jesus I root up all malice, bitterness and roots of destruction from my life. I release the fire of God against these plantings."

(2) "In the name of Jesus I destroy with the hammer of the Word all constructions of household witchcraft in my marriage and my family."
(Name those things personal to you as the Holy Spirit brings them back to your memory.)

Repeat: "Be destroyed in the name of Jesus." Keep going until the Spirit brings confirmation that things are beginning to break.

As you wait on the Spirit you can pray in the Spirit.

NB: Elements of deliverance praying can be repetitive but as you become more skilled you will find it less so because the power of your authority increases.

Figuratively, you can use other elements like the:-

- Sword of the Spirit to cut away and dissect a problem.
- axe to remove tenacious weeds from your ground
- the wind to scatter
- hailstones to pound the enemy

> - sun by day and the moon by night to smite the opponent
> - stone of David to bring down giants of provocation in your life
>
> These are some of the weapons you can use effectively to dismantle and destroy all work of evil. Search the Word for other weapons and learn how to use then resourcefully and skillfully.

Remember the prayer above is an example. You will model your prayers and the areas unique to your situation against it. It is a basic structure for you to work with. As the Spirit trains you, other ways suitable to you will emerge from your discipline. So keep going and expand your territory of authority in prayer.

You may need to read the Word and pray in the Spirit for a reasonable length of time to begin to feel a clear head.

8.1   MEDITATIVE SPIRIT

"Let the words of my mouth and the meditation of my heart be acceptable in your sight, O LORD, my Rock and my Redeemer," (Psalms 19:14 ESV).

We come into His presence waiting in stillness knowing that He is God. Silence is a golden moment before the feet of Jesus. Just wait on Him. Love Him and just call His name "Jesus." It is holy quietness when we are waiting before The Presence for His favour and love to be bestowed upon us. Listen to Him and let Him speak in the silence of your doting spirit. It is a healing and rejuvenating experience to be in His presence. Stay before your Lord and have these precious moments of intimacy with Him. It is healing and refreshing.

8.2   IN GOD'S PRESENCE

Be dutiful in your prayer life. Learn to pray more frequently in the Spirit so it becomes second nature to you. When praying in the spirit becomes a way of life, you will incorporate it into daily chores. You can be sitting on a bus, washing the dishes, mowing the lawn and doing so many other household chores whilst praying quietly in the spirit. That is praying without ceasing, as you are always preoccupied with the things of God. No time for gossiping and meddling in other people's affairs. When you are mindful always of the things pertaining to the kingdom of God you will find you have few friends as people find you a tad reserved.

Do not give in to the social pressures to be busy and stressed keeping up with the demands of life. Whilst we have to live with life's distractions, always find time to be with God. Jesus often sought to escape to a place of solitude, away from the multitudes to be alone with God. It is a Spirit initiated call, and we know when the Spirit is prompting us to be alone with God. There is no greater experience of longing to be in His presence. Lovingly, God will cause you always to want to be in His presence and the fruits of effective praying will in time yield a fruitfully abundant harvest.

References:

(1) Barnes' Commentary Notes on 2 Corinthians 2:10
(2) Young's Concordance
(3) Health Encyclopedia (URMC)